GW00362781

The
WISDOM
of the Vikings

Compiled by Nicholas Jones

edda uk
Cambridge
2005

Published by edda uk ltd.
Cambridge

© edda uk 2005
© Translations Nicholas Jones
© Introduction Nicholas Jones

Design: Helgi Hilmarsson

ISBN 1-904945-00-7

Contents

Publisher's Note

The Wisdom series is intended for the general reader. These books are intended to open up a little window on the past through which readers may catch a tantalising glimpse of ancient cultures. We hope that this will encourage people to go further and get to know these cultures and their histories better. Every effort has been made to create books that readers will find interesting and enjoyable, applying the highest standards in both the production of the text and the design and presentation.

By comparing the books in the Wisdom series, readers will see how the same idea often turns up at different times and places, only dressed in different clothing. The Celts chose other ways to express themselves than the Romans; the men of the North do not always speak like those of the Mediterranean. In many cases it is the literary tradition of a particular culture that determines the form of the text and sets its own mark on a familiar idea.

By bringing these classic texts to a modern audience in a new version, we hope that readers will gain an insight into the glories of the past, and that these glories will live on to inspire new generations of readers, both young and old.

Forth I bear
From the wordshrine
Glory timber
Green with language.

Þat ber'k út
ór orðhofi
mærðar timbr
máli laufgat.

Egill Skallagrímsson Sonatorrek 5

Egill is composing in honour of his dead son. The
wordshrine is his mind or his heart, where he tends the
precious gift of poetry that will keep his son's name
alive and make it flourish.

Good
Advice

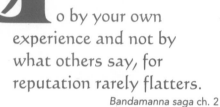

o by your own experience and not by what others say, for reputation rarely flatters.

Bandamanna saga ch. 2

There are things you should be wary of and shun like the devil himself – drinking, board games, whores, quarrelling, and gambling. For on such foundations are the greatest calamities built; and unless they strive to avoid them, very few are able to live long without blame or sin.

King's Mirror ch. 4

A man must be able
  To ask and to reply
If he wants to be called clever;
  Tell one your thoughts
  But two never,
What's known to three is known to all.

Hávamál 63

10

vil people are
best known only by
hearsay.

Hœnsa-Thóris saga ch. 6

 oorer it is
  Than people say,
Ale for mortal men,
  For the longer you drink
  The less you retain
Mastery of your mind.

Hávamál 12

The mistrust of alcohol is expressed
most succinctly in Grettis saga ch. 19:
'Ale is a different person.'

 nly agree to today what you won't regret tomorrow.

Bandamanna saga ch. 10

No one should count on
A cornfield sown early
Nor too soon their son;
Weather makes harvests
And wits make sons,
Each subject to circumstance.

Hávamál 88

tem the river at
its source.

Snorri Sturluson *Edda:*
Skáldskaparmál 26

The proverb obviously has a general
application, but Snorri uses it more
literally: it is put into the mouth of
the god Thor in one of his coarser
myths, when he is in danger of being
swept away by a torrent caused by a
giantess urinating into a river he is
crossing.

Human Nature

 obody learns
from other people's
mistakes.

Thorsteins tháttr stangarhöggs

There are few who
recall your better deeds
when they know your worse.

Njáls saga ch. 139

In the words of Mark Antony, in
Shakespeare's Julius Caesar III. ii:
    'The evil that men do lives after them,
    The good is oft interred with their bones.'

No man is his own creation.

Grettis saga ch. 41

In the context of the saga, Grettir's comment is double-edged: first, that people are not necessarily made the way they would choose; and second, that no one can escape the demands of Fate.

Everyone has their
own particular merit.

Njáls saga ch. 77

In the context of the saga, the proverb
is deeply ironic: it is said by the hero
Gunnarr of Hlíðarendi to his wicked
wife Hallgerðr after she refuses him
two strands of her hair to make a
bowstring that will save his life.

 gift always looks for something in return.

Gísla saga ch. 15

Anger does not
look with eyes of truth.

Fóstbrœðra saga ch. 22

The same warning appears in Sturla
Thórðarson's *Íslendinga saga*: 'An
angry man's words are not to be
heeded.'

The unwise man
   Lies awake all night
Anxiously tossing and turning;
   When morning comes
   He is careworn still
And his burdens as bad as ever.

Hávamál 23

People always notice what is far away, not what is right under their noses.

Heiðarvíga saga ch. 14

In other words, people are always minding other people's business rather than their own.

Family and Friends

Bare is a man's
back with no brother
to protect it.

Njáls saga ch. 152

The proverb is quoted in other
sagas, e.g. *Grettis saga* ch. 82.

A son is better
  Though born late on
After the fall of his father;
  Few memorial stones
  Stand by the wayside
Save raised by kin to kin.

Hávamál 72

The nose is near to the eyes.

Njáls saga ch. 12

The sense is that people need to take responsibility for the actions of other members of their family. In this case, the chieftain Höskuldr is being urged by his brother Hrútr to offer compensation for a man killed at the instigation of his daughter, Hallgerðr. Hrútr goes on to say: 'We need to put an end to all evil talk and compensate him for his son and so save your daughter's reputation.'

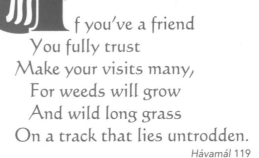

If you've a friend
  You fully trust
Make your visits many,
  For weeds will grow
  And wild long grass
On a track that lies untrodden.

Hávamál 119

31

Times past I was young
And travelled alone,
Alone I lost my way;
I felt myself rich
When I found another –
Man is man's delight.

Hávamál 47

orrow eats the heart
if you some time never tell
to anyone all your thoughts.

Hávamál 121

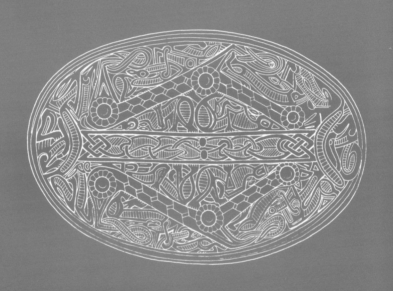

Man and
Woman

A maiden's words
No man should trust
Nor yet what women say;
For on a shifting wheel
Were shaped their hearts,
Deceit set in their breast.

Hávamál 84

 luntly now I speak,
  For both sides I know –
False are men's minds to women;
  We fairest speak
  When our aims are foulest,
To tempt their tender hearts.

Hávamál 91

Avoid impropriety,
both in a maiden's love or
with another man's wife; such
things lead to trouble.

Völsunga saga ch. 21

There is a sad irony in these words, which
come from a speech of advice by Brynhildr
when she first meets the hero Sigurðr. Sigurðr
betroths himself to Brynhildr but then marries
the princess Guðrún, so initiating the central
catastrophe of the saga.

In an enchantress's arms
   Choose never to sleep,
So she locks you in her limbs;
   Her wiles are such
   You'll soon neglect
Your public duty and prince's words.
   You'll refuse your food,
   Find no pleasure in others,
And go sorrowful to sleep.

Hávamál 113-4

The word translated 'enchantress' means both a witch
and a woman skilled in many arts. It is perhaps
interesting that the danger of sleeping with such a
woman is not that it is bad; rather, it is so good that it
distracts men from 'more important' matters.

The eyes cannot conceal it if a woman loves a man.

Gunnlaugs saga ch. 11

A verse said to be by Gunnlaugr about the thwarted love between himself and Helga the Fair begins with the words: 'Woman was born for discord.'

irl talk often
ends in trouble.

Gísla saga ch. 9

The words are those of Gísli's wife,
Auðr. Thorkell has just overheard his
wife, Ásgerðr, admitting her fondness
for Gísli's friend Vésteinn. The
resulting jealousies set off the events
that lead to the deaths of all the main
characters, including Gísli himself.

Wisdom
and
Knowledge

I suggest we leave this
matter to the wiser among
us; for the more fools you get
agreeing on something the
worse their advice is likely to
turn out.

Laxdœla saga ch. 21

The words are ascribed to Ólafr the Peacock.
Ólafr, the magnificent hero of the first part
of the saga, was the son of an Icelandic
chieftain and an Irish princess slave.

No better burden
  Can you bear to the road
Than a great weight of wisdom;
  Stronger than riches
  In a strange place it proves,
The refuge of the wretched.

Hávamál 10

Good advice should be followed, wherever it comes from.

Bandamanna saga ch. 10

can pay attention
to the steering and still
think of other things.

Grœnlendinga saga ch. 3

The words are those of Leif the Lucky, the
son of Erik the Red, and addressed to his
crew who do not understand why he is
sailing against the wind; Leif had seen
some sailors shipwrecked on a reef, and it
was his rescue of them that earned him his
nickname.

No one is a complete fool if he knows how to hold his tongue.

Grettis saga ch. 88

That summer Erik went to settle the land he had found and called it Greenland, because he said that people would be keener to move there if it had an attractive name.

Eiríks saga rauða ch. 2

Like any modern advertiser or spin-doctor, Erik the Red was clearly aware of the importance of image. According to the *Book of Settlements*, Iceland was given its name by the 9th-century explorer, Raven-Flóki, who spent one wretched winter there before returning to Norway with nothing good to say about the place.

oderate-wise
Each man should be,
Never too much should he know;
The happiest lives
Are had by those
Whose learning knows proper limits.

Hávamál 54

Y ou can forgive people for sometimes getting things wrong, but there's no excusing the man who won't believe the truth when he sees it with his own eyes.

Fóstbrœðra saga ch. 23

Freedom, Independence and Alienation

etter a humble
House than none,
A man's his own master at home;
A pair of goats
And a patched roof
At least are better than begging.

Hávamál 37

he worst things
are those that are
suffered alone.

Grettis saga ch. 16

e not a shoemaker
Nor a shaft-smith
Except for yourself alone:
If the shoe is ill-made
Or the shaft is crooked
Then you'll have all hell to pay.

Hávamál 126

veryone has to
travel farthest with
themselves.

Gísla saga ch. 14

he entry to a king's court is wide, the way out narrow.

Egils saga ch. 68

The words are those of the wise counsellor, Arinbjörn, who mediates between his friend Egill and his king and Egill's archenemy, Erik Bloodaxe.

eep moving on,
You cannot stay
Always in only one place:
Loved becomes loathed
If too long you sit
At the hearth of another's home.

Hávamál 35

Conflict
and
Reconciliation

He knows all who
knows moderation.

Gísla saga ch. 15

In a world where the least offence was
viewed as an affront to a man's honour and
credibility, and therefore demanded instant
vengeance, self-restraint was vital to
survival. Moderation and knowing one's
limits is a recurrent theme in the sagas.

The greater the vengeance the longer it takes.

Ljósvetninga saga ch. 13

It is a scandal and a shame to see men hurling insults at each other here, whether it is our men or others; there is nothing to be gained by this and it leads only to trouble. The way we should be talking is the way that might best lead to reconciliation.

Heiðarvíga saga ch. 37

Do not bandy words with ignorant men in public places; they often say worse things than they realise, and you get called a coward and they believe that this is true. Wait till the next day and then kill them and pay them for their slanders.

Völsunga saga ch. 21

 he starved
louse has a sharp
bite.

Book of Settlements ch. 49

He who gives warning is not the cause.

Fljótsdœla saga ch. 23

The saga calls this an 'old proverb'.
The meaning is something like
'The bearer of a warning should not
be held to blame', and so perhaps
'Don't shoot the messenger'.

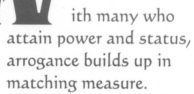

With many who attain power and status, arrogance builds up in matching measure.

Snorri Sturluson *Heimskringla: Saga of Magnús the Good* ch. 7

ur land shall be
built on law and not
destroyed through
anarchy.

Njáls saga ch. 70

The first part of the quotation – 'Með
lögum skal land byggja' – is the motto
of modern Iceland.

Honour, Truth and Trust

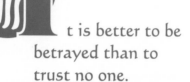

It is better to be
betrayed than to
trust no one.

Fljótsdœla saga ch. 13

If you have a friend
Who you don't fully trust
But still want something of him,
Be fair in speech
But false in thought,
Treat disloyalty with lies.

Hávamál 45

We are now in a dilemma: disgrace if we do nothing, and dubious honour if we look to put things right.

Víga-Glúms saga ch. 11

It is better to have brief dignity than long-lasting ignominy.

Laxdœla saga ch. 21

He lies well who lies with witnesses.

Thorsteins saga Síðu Hallssonar ch. 3

 loyal few
provide a safer defence
for a king than a
multitude of traitors.

Saxo Grammaticus
Gesta Danorum V. iii. 14

Trust no one so well that you trust not yourself better. There are many that are best treated with caution.

Grettis saga ch. 67

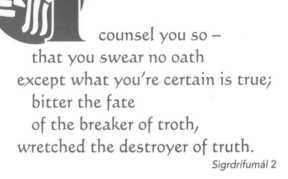 counsel you so –
that you swear no oath
except what you're certain is true;
   bitter the fate
   of the breaker of troth,
wretched the destroyer of truth.

Sigrdrífumál 2

79

Courage, Fate, and Death

Something will turn up to save a man whose hour is not yet come.

Fóstbrœðra saga ch. 23

The same idea is found in *Sverris saga*: 'No one can kill a man who is not fated nor save a man who is.'

 fool believes
He'll live forever
By steering clear of strife;
But age gives him
No grant of peace,
Though spears may spare his life.

Hávamál 16

The lame can ride a horse,
The handless herd his flocks,
The deaf can do deeds of valour;
    Better be blind
    Than burned on a pyre,
A corpse is no use to you.

Hávamál 71

84

attle die,
    Kinsmen die,
Yourself you'll die the same;
    I know but this
    That never dies:
Reputation in posterity.

Hávamál 77

Deyr fé,
    Deyja frændr,
    Deyr sjálfr it sama.
Ek veit einn
    At aldrei deyr:
    Dómr um dauðan hvern.

Courage means more
Than the might of the sword
When fierce men face each other;
For a valiant man
May victory win
However blunt his blade.

Fáfnismál 30

The idea appears many times in Viking writings,
perhaps nowhere more succinctly than in Völsunga
saga ch. 19: 'A good heart is better than a sharp
sword.'

As often as not it isn't the bigger party that wins the day if people stand up to it with boldness and resolution.

Færeyinga saga ch. 19

We have two choices before us: either to gain victory like men, however unlikely this may be against such a foe, or to fall like true warriors with heads held high, and that is better than to live in shame, afraid to defend the honour of our king.

Bjarnar saga Hítdœlakappa ch. 4

A similar expression of heroism in battle appears in *Jómsvíkinga saga* ch. 37: 'To me it seems a good thing to die with fame and glory; but your life will be a humiliation to you, for you will live in shame and skulk your way towards death.'

e have won great renown
Whether we die now or tomorrow;
No one outlives the night
Laid down by the Fates.'

There fell Sörli
At the front gable
And Hamðir sank
At the hall back.

Hamðismál 30-1

The Viking 'Fates' are the Norns, who myths told wove
the tapestry of men's lives.

Money
and
Wealth

The rich sons' folds
  Stood full of sheep,
They bear now the beggar's staff;
  Wealth can be
  Like the blinking of an eye,
The most fickle of friends.

Hávamál 78

Lots of eyes start squinting when there's money around.

Bandamanna saga ch. 5

With the wealth
  You've won yourself
Do not scrimp and spare;
  What's meant for a friend
  A foe may take,
Good plans can go awry.

Hávamál 40

If you have a lot of capital invested in trade, divide it into three parts. Put one third into partnerships with men who are permanently established in market towns, who you can trust, and who are experienced in business. Divide the rest between different places and ventures, for if your money is invested in many places at once, this minimises the risk of your losing all your wealth in one go.

King's Mirror ch. 4

 ean clothes
can often conceal
strong arms.

Saxo Grammaticus *Gesta
Danorum* VI. vi. 3

It is in all men's natures to get rid of any stolen goods they have in their possession as quickly as they can.

Njáls saga ch. 49

The Wisdom of the Vikings

Other people's eyes

'From the fury of the Northmen, O Lord, deliver us' the monks are said to have chanted. Whatever the truth of this – the records date from well after the Viking Age – the prayer pretty much sums up the reaction of western Europe to the sacking of the monastery on Lindisfarne in 793 and subsequent mayhem: fear, horror and incomprehension.

Not entirely unreasonably, the Vikings got a bad press. The only people who could read and write in the places where they turned up as unwelcome visitors were men of the Church. The Church was rich and relatively undefended and an obvious target. The Vikings, at this period anyway, were heathens, and illiterate. In the propaganda war there was only ever going to be one winner.

There is certainly no reason to think that the Vikings introduced anything particularly new in the way of nastiness into Europe – in the years before their arrival, Christians had been raiding other Christians, Christians and Moslems fighting each other in Spain and southern France, Charlemagne converting the Saxons by the simple means of slaughtering them to a man. Only, the Vikings were new in themselves, a bolt from the blue, arriving and disappearing without warning, something unfamiliar and random and therefore terrifying.

Many theories have been put forward to explain why the Vikings appeared at the time they did, but one factor is beyond dispute: technology. In the years leading up to the Viking Age, along the coasts of Norway and among the islands of Denmark, the people of Scandinavia had perfected their ships and the art of navigation[1]. Now it was time to use them. In any way they could – trading, raiding, settling, a bit of one here, a bit of another there. It is very unlikely that the Northmen distinguished between these activities quite as clearly as we might today. They were just interested in whatever might turn in a profit.

In their own words
The Vikings probably didn't think of themselves as being particularly vicious; we have no way of knowing, since they couldn't write back to their accusers. They knew how to carve runes, and the Viking Age saw a huge explosion of such inscriptions, particularly in Sweden. But they tend to say little more than 'Helgi is buried here' or 'Valdimar went to Russia and fed the eagles well' (i.e. killed lots of people). Which does not get us very far.

So how can we know what these men thought about themselves and life in general? The people of the North inherited a stock of heroic tales common to all the Germanic peoples – stories and names from the Edda poems also turn up in Old English works such as *Beowulf* [2]. To these they added stories of their own, passing them on by word of mouth, adding bits here, losing bits there as the generations went by. These poems defined their traditional history, their religion, their outlook on life, and their very nature.

During the Viking years they developed a second and very different form of poetry – skaldic verse – dealing with specific people and events. This, too, was passed on by word of mouth, but unlike the traditional poetry was

[1] If you find yourself in Oslo, go to the Viking Ship Museum and marvel at the grace and elegance of the Gokstad ship.

[2] The 'Edda' and other terms used here are explained in the glossary of Terms, Works and Authors.

probably not subject to significant change in transmission due to the complexity of its verse forms. This, together with the stories that would have gone with it, kept alive memories of real kings and real events.

All this is typical of any preliterate people.

Around the year 1000, the people of the North accepted Christianity, and with Christianity came, little by little, the art of writing. But then something remarkable happened. When the rest of Europe was brought within the Christian fold it also adopted the accepted literary traditions of the Catholic Church – its forms of writing (sermons, saints' lives and the like) and its language, Latin. But not so in the North. Or, at least, not in the colony of Iceland that had been settled in the years around 900 and had long acted as the storehouse of the Viking cultural heritage. When the Icelanders started writing, they did so in their own language and using material from their own native stock, first their own history and the history of the kings of Norway, and then, in the 13th century, an extraordinary literary outpouring of sagas, traditional poetry and all manner of other writings. The vast majority of the quotations in this book come from 13th century Icelandic texts.

The question has to be asked, How much can these texts tell us about the Vikings, who had ceased to be a force in European politics after the defeat of Haraldr harðráði, king of Norway, by Harold Godwinsson at Stamford Bridge in Yorkshire in 1066?[3] The answer is, happily, quite a lot. A lot of the skaldic verse is definitely from the Viking Age,

[3] Though of course William the Bastard of Normandy was himself of Norse descent, Normandy, as its name suggests, having been granted to Viking settlers by Charles the Simple, king of France, in 911. But by 1066 the Normans had been thoroughly 'frenchified'. On William's name, all contemporary records call him William the Bastard, even his tombstone! The epithet 'the Conqueror' does not appear before about 1300.

and we have every reason to believe that many of the Edda poems go back that far, if not further.

This traditional material, carefully preserved and nurtured, without any doubt at all had a profound influence on how the Icelanders viewed events from their own history and pervade the ways they put them into written form in their sagas. Here and there the sagas give glimpses of a later age, the age in which they were written. But for the most part the view they present of the world is identical to that found in the poetry, and that is the world of the Vikings.

The Viking world

Before we try to generalise too much about the Vikings we need to remember that the Viking Age lasted over 250 years, during which there were many changes, not least among the people of the North themselves. The earliest raids were on a small scale, two or three ships probably manned entirely by men from a single area under the leadership of a local chieftain. By 1015, Knútr (Canute) was a sophisticated Christian king with a literate bureaucracy and a large, organised army, ruling an empire that covered England, Denmark and Norway.

Inevitably, trade and settlement brought the Vikings into closer contact with the world outside and they were generally only too ready to adopt new customs and ideas, most obviously in religion. Within their homelands, too, there were huge political and social changes. At the beginning of the Viking Age the North was at heart a collection of more or less independent small states whose allegiance to any more distant overlord was very tenuous. By the end of the period the states of Norway, Denmark, Sweden and Gautland (modern southern Sweden) were fully defined, with power centralised under kings who looked outwards to the other kings of Europe rather than inwards to their own people.

Even so, certain consistent features do emerge. Obviously there is the interest in battle and heroism, but this is hardly unique to the Vikings. In other respects, the mental world of the Vikings, in particular as represented in Hávamál, strikes us as being peculiarly modern. The mobility that came with ships and trade, and especially the settlements, disrupted the existing social units, leading to both an increased emphasis on the individual and an almost desperate clinging to the traditional backbone of society, the family.

The literature shows little sign of a sense of society in the abstract. There is, however, evidence of considerable social mobility, with poor men making good and achieving power and influence and people of longstanding hereditary power sinking into obscurity. In both the heathen and Christian periods religion appears to have had only very limited influence on Viking thinking – certainly nothing in comparison to the pervasive awareness of fate and the uncertainties of fortune.

The quotations collected here give us a glimpse into the minds of the Vikings themselves, the things that preoccupied them and how they felt people should deal with them. The overriding theme is one of personal responsibility – the individual has to rely on himself, for he cannot rely on others. Indeed, there is often a sense of mistrust of others; however much they may seem to provide support they are liable to fail you in your hour of need. A man has to find his own way in life, aided only by the

powers he was born with and can develop for himself –
intelligence, knowledge and cunning; personal honour and
integrity; reputation in this world and after death;
moderation and a willingness to compromise; a spirit of
adventure that will drive you on to seek new places and
opportunities; and courage and an indomitable spirit that
will not surrender, even when all hope is gone.

Some Hints on Pronunciation

Most names in the text are given in their Old Norse forms,
except that th has been substituted for the original letter þ
(pronounced as the th in think), which many people find
confusing. Otherwise the following hints on pronunciation
may be helpful:

ð   like *th* in *with, mother*
j   like the *y* sound in *yes, few*
s   always like the *s* in *horse*, never as in *rose*
r   trilled as in Italian or Spanish. The *r* that appears after
    consonants at the end of some names marks the
    nominative case; if you don't like it, just ignore it.

The acute accent on vowels, e.g. á and ú, meant that the
vowel was long.

Terms, Works and Authors

Bandamanna saga ('The Saga of the Confederates') Short saga set in the north of Iceland, unusual in taking a broadly comic and satirical view of life.

Bjarnar saga Hítdœlakappa ('The Saga of Bjorn Champion of Hitardalers') Biographical saga set in western Iceland and at the court of Norway, telling the life of the poet Björn and how a false friend cheats him of his beloved Oddný.

Book of Settlements (*Landnámabók*) List of the settlers of Iceland c.870-c.930, with details of their land claims and descendants, compiled early in the 13th century. It also records a number of early traditions, including on several disputes that are treated in greater detail in the sagas.

Edda 1. A collection of around 30 traditional poems made in Iceland around 1250. The eddic poems are anonymous, generally fairly simple in style, and either recount stories or record ancient wisdom. The poems fall into two groups. The mythological group includes poems telling some of the adventures of Thor and other gods; the famous *Völuspá* ('The Sibyl's Prophecy'), which describes the origins of the world and its eventual destruction; and *Hávamál* (see separate entry). Most of the best poetry is in the heroic group, which centres around the 'Nibelung' legend, the story used by the composer Richard Wagner in his 'Ring Cycle'. Themes from the Edda have been much plundered by J. R. R. Tolkien and other writers of fantasy. 2. See **Snorri Sturluson**.

Egill Skallagrímsson (c.900-c.980) Generally regarded as the greatest of the Norse *skálds*, from the west of Iceland. His poetical remains include individual verses on incidents from his life; *Höfuðlausn* ('Head Ransom'), supposedly composed after his capture by his enemy Erik Bloodaxe, king of York – the story goes that Erik was so impressed that he let Egill go; and the elegies *Sonatorrek*, to his drowned son Böðvarr, and *Arinbjarnarkviða*, to his friend Arinbjörn. Egill's life and much of his poetry is recorded in a long saga, *Egils saga*.

Eiríks saga rauða ('The Saga of Erik the Red') Saga describing the turbulent life of a man banished first from Norway and then from Iceland. It describes the settlement of Greenland, led by Erik, and some of the early Viking journeys to the continent of North America.

Færeyinga saga ('The Saga of the Faeroe Islanders') Saga describing a feud on the Faeroe Islands, between Shetland and Iceland. In the character of Thrándr of Gata it contains one of the finest anti-heroes in world literature.

Fáfnismál One of the heroic poems of the Edda, telling how the hero Sigurðr slew the dragon Fáfnir and won his gold.

Fljótsdœla saga Late saga set in the east of Iceland.

Fóstbrœðra saga ('The Saga of the Sworn Brothers') Saga starting in northwest Iceland and ending in Norway. The first part recounts the adventures of two young yobs, the aggressive Thorgeirr and the delightful Thormóðr, who spends much of his time mooning after unsuitable girls. Thormóðr eventually dies a hero's death fighting on the side of St. Olaf, king of Norway, in 1030.

Gísla saga ('The Saga of Gísli') One of the most beautiful of the sagas, set in the northwest of Iceland, full of mystery and irony. It tells of the poet Gísli, who is outlawed and has to live in isolation, tormented by terrifying dreams prefiguring his death. In Gísli's wife Auðr the saga contains one of the most memorable and rounded female characters in medieval, or any, literature.

Grettis saga ('The Saga of Grettir the Strong') Long saga telling the life of Iceland's most famous outlaw. Apart from his strength and resilience, Grettir has many fine qualities but is fated to suffer from recurrent ill luck and a debilitating fear of the dark.

Grœnlendinga saga ('The Saga of the Greenlanders') Semi-historical saga set largely in Greenland. Along with *Eiríks saga rauða* it provides us with much of our knowledge of the Viking exploration of North America and attempts to settle there.

Gunnlaugs saga ormstungu ('The Saga of Gunnlaug Serpent-Tongue') Elegant and rather romantic saga about the poet Gunnlaugr, who is cheated of his beloved Helga the Fair while working abroad. It contains several verses by Gunnlaugr and other poets.

Hákonarmál Elegy by the Norwegian skáld Eyvindr Finnsson composed on the death of Earl Hákon, ruler of Norway from 986 to 995. Hákon appears to have fostered a late flowering of the Viking heathendom, in opposition to the Christianity favoured by the Norwegian royal family, whom he had temporarily ousted.

Hamðismál Powerful and probably very ancient heroic poem from the Edda collection. It tells of two brothers, Hamðir and Sörli, who are sent by their mother on a hopeless mission to avenge their sister, brutally killed by her husband Jörmunrekkr (the historical Ermanaric, king of the Ostrogoths, who died c.375).

Hávamál ('The Sayings of the High One') The longest poem in the Edda collection. To call *Hávamál* a 'poem' is something of a misnomer: its second half clearly consists of fragments from several different poems, and its first half is an anthology of traditional wisdom verses on a wide range of subjects. The collection is given an overall frame by being ascribed to 'the High One' (i.e. the

Further reading

The complete sagas of the Icelanders are available in translation in the
Penguin Classics series and individual sagas are published in various other
series, e.g. Everyman and Oxford World Classics. Perhaps those most likely
to appeal to modern readers are *Gísla saga, Færeyinga saga* and *Laxdœla saga*;
Njáls saga is best left until readers have some familiarity with saga style.
Older – for instance 19th-century – translations are best avoided: they tend to
be done in a pseudo-archaic style that gives a very false impression of the
colloquial language of the originals.

There are no really satisfactory translations of the Edda poems but among the
more reliable are those of Henry Adams Bellows, Lee M. Hollander, and
Carolyne Larrington, all called *The Poetic Edda*.

The most readable parts of Snorri Sturluson's Edda are translated in:
Anthony Faulkes *Snorri Sturluson: Edda*.
Jean I. Young *The Prose Edda: Tales from Norse Mythology*.

For a good general introduction to the sagas as literature, see:
Peter Hallberg *The Icelandic Saga*.
Originally published in 1897 but reprinted many times and still very readable,
though inevitably out of date in some respects, is:
W. P. Ker *Epic and Romance*.

For Viking mythology, see:
H. R. Ellis Davidson *Gods and Myths of Northern Europe*.
R. I. Page *Norse Myths*.
E. O. G. Turville-Petre *Myth and Religion of the North*.

For Viking history:
Peter Foote and David M. Wilson *The Viking Achievement*.
J. Graham-Campbell and D. Kidd *The Vikings* (British Museum Publications).
Gwyn Jones *A History of the Vikings*.
R. I. Page *Chronicles of the Vikings* (British Museum Publications).
Peter Sawyer, ed. *The Oxford Illustrated History of the Vikings*.
Jacqueline Simpson *Everyday Life in the Viking Age*.

There is a good BBC website on the Vikings:
www.bbc.co.uk/history/ancient/vikings/